MW00900570

GURU GIRL

RECIPE BOOK

Smoothies and Energy Bites

Andrea Noemi Bredak

Copyright © 2019. Andrea Noemi Bredak

All rights reserved.

ISBN : 978-1-0871-0174-3

" LET FOOD BE THY MEDICINE ,

THY MEDICINE SHALL BE THY FOOD . "

- HIPPOCRATES -

" WE ALL BECOME WHAT WE EAT ,
HOW WE THINK ,
WHAT WE SPEAK .
THE POWER OF MIND IS VERY STRONG .
IT CAN BUILD OR DESTROY .
MEDITATION AND DAILY PRAYERS CAN CLEAN
THE MIND AND PURIFY THE SOUL .
CHOOSE YOUR MEALS CONSCIOUSLY
NOT DRASTICALLY .
ADDING MORE RAW FRUITS AND VEGETABLES
IN YOUR LIFE WILL FULLY BENEFIT
YOUR BODY AND MIND . "

- ANDREA NOEMI BREDAK -

DEDICATION

LOVE , FAITH , TRUST AND SURRENDER .
I DEDICATE THIS BOOK :

TO GOD ,

TO A SPECIAL PERSON MY PARTNER ,

MY FAMILY ,

FRIENDS ,

TO THE WORLD . "

- A.N.B. -

CONTENTS

I. ACKNOWLEDGEMENT

There is so much to be grateful for and so many people to thank.

God (our Creator, Higher power) has guided me and has provided many blessings, people and events which have changed my life.

Without Him I am nothing, with Him I am everything.

My purpose in life is to be present in every moment and use this opportunity to serve others.

This journey would not be possible without an amazing partner, my man who loves and supports me.

Lastly, the greatest influence in writing this book has been my Hungarian family and culture with our unique style, food and spices.

Thank you God ,

I am grateful for all your appearances
in all shape and time ,

Grateful for all challenges ,
Hard lessons ,
Funny jokes ,

You're Omnipresence and Love .

II. INTRODUCTION

We are all searching for an easy solution to a strong, healthy body, mind and soul.
The purpose of this book is to introduce a simple and easy guide for a vibrant health.
In the following pages are my personal recipes and remedies to maximize your physical and spiritual health, flexibility and increase your energy.
All this recipes are raw, vegan and organic.
They provide maximum nutrition, vitamins, minerals and protein.
These are the necessary supplements for cleansing, detoxification, high energy and workouts.

My simple step by step instructions and recipes will assure your success and maintain your motivation regardless of your circumstances.
Based on my extensive experience with public school adolescences,
Montessori School pre K students,
Assisted Living Facilities residents,
private group yoga, dance and meditation classes on Hollywood Beach,
customized client meal plans and raw-vegan-organic food

products at my Guru Girl Store in the Yellow and Green Farmers market.
I have created these recipes and have witnessed the transformation in those who are willing to adhere to these simple and effective program.

III. HOUSEHOLD SUPPLIES

" YOUR DIET IS A BANK ACCOUNT.
GOOD FOOD CHOICES ARE
GOOD INVESTMENT. "

- BETHENNY FRANKEL -

* Wax papers
* Measuring cup
* Mastering spoons
* A good blender
* Ice cream scoop
* Allforhome rectangle 12 mold
* Food processor
* Lemon/lime squeezer
* Lemon/ginger greater

IV. HEALTHY SUBSTITUTIONS

" ANY FOOD THAT REQUIRES ENHANCING BY

THE USE OF CHEMICAL SUBSTANCES

SHOULD IN NO WAY BE CONSIDERED

A FOOD. "

- JOHN H. TOBE -

FRUITS & VEGETABLES

Unhealthy/ * Canned food & concentrated juices
(full of sugar, colors, artificial flavors and chemicals)

Healthy Choices/
* Organic, fresh, non GMO
 (eat them, juice them fresh or frozen)

FATS

Animal based/
* Butter, cream, milk, yoghurt, creamer
    * Read the labels and do your research
        (before you purchase them)
    *Make sure it is farm raised with love
        (non caged or treated with hormones)
    *Anything you can not pronounce mostly bad for you :
preservatives, colors, chemicals, sugar, artificial flavors etc.

Plant based, good fats/
* Avocado

* Seeds & Nuts
* Cold pressed oils
(healthy lifestyle+easy digestion+better absorption)

OILS

* Coconut, hemp, chia, flax, avocado, sesami oils
   (cold pressed, amber colored glass bottle)

Plant based MILK & CREAMER
(You can make your own)

* Hemp, almond, cashew, flax milk, yoghurt and creamer

SWEETENERS

Unhealthy Sweeteners : Watch out and do your research!

* Table or white sugar (Sucrose)
* High fructose corn syrup

(Sodas/Desserts/Cereals)
* Acesulfame Potassium
(Sunett, Sweet One)
* Aspartame (Equal, Nutra Sweet)
* Sucralose (Splenda)

Healthy upgrade : All natural

There is always an option to find a solution.

* Raw, unfiltered honey
* Date & date sugar & date syrup
* Coconut sugar
* Organic A grade Maple syrup
* Figs

PROTEIN POWDERS

Some treated with harmful chemicals, preservatives, artificial flavors, colors, sugar, corn syrup, corn starch.

There is always a better alternatives

to choose wisely a nutritious meal.

Such as a PLANT based, all natural,
non GMO, protein powder :

- Evolve
- SunWarrior
- Plant Fusion
- Vega One
- Vegan
- VegaProtein

CHOCOLATE

The difference between Cocoa and raw Cacao

COCOA : is roasted at high temperature
(milk chocolate, cookies, ice cream etc.)

CACAO (raw) :

cold-pressed, un-roasted, has living enzymes, no fat
(raw, vegan, dark chocolate)

Provides a cleaner, healthier and vibrant life.

OATS

There are always some products at the markets treated with sugar, chemicals, artificial flavors, colors and chemicals.
It is your responsibility to read the labels and do some research about what you put in to your system.

The healthy version is all raw, unprocessed and plain.

Healthy Oats :

- Whole Food Organic
- Better Oats
- Food to Live
- Nature's Path
- Publix Green Wise etc .

V. RECIPE INGREDIENTS

" IF YOU KEEP GOOD FOOD IN YOUR FRIDGE,

YOU WILL EAT GOOD FOOD. "

- Errick McAdams -

Fruits
* Apple, banana, cherry, coconut water, cranberry, dates, goji berry, grapes, lemon, lime, mango, mixed frozen berries, pineapple, raisin , raspberry, watermelon

Vegetables
* Avocado, carrots, very, cilantro, cucumber, ginger, kale, mint, parsley, spinach

Spices
* Cayenne pepper, cinnamon, pink Himalayan salt, turmeric, vanilla extra

Oils
* Hemp, coconut oil

Sweeteners
* Barley malt, coconut sugar, honey (optional), maple syrup, shredded coconut

Seeds and Nuts
(all raw)

* Almond, flax seeds (grounded), hemp seeds, oats (quick), peanuts, pistachio (shelled), pumpkin seeds, sunflower seeds, walnuts

Others

* Dark, vegan chocolate chips
(Whole Food Store),

* Protein Powder (vegan, plant based, your favorite, healthy choice)

" JUICES OF FRUITS AND VEGETABLES ARE
PURE GIFTS FROM MOTHER NATURE
AND THE MOST NATURAL WAY TO HEAL
YOUR BODY AND MAKE YOURSELF
WHOLE AGAIN. "

- FARNOOSH BROCK -

VI. GURU GIRL HEALTHY RECIPES

How to guide your body to purify?

* Drink 6-8 glasses of water daily

* Chew your food min. 25-30 times, mix it well with your saliva

* Eat clean, raw or steamed fresh fruits and vegetables

* Detox your entire system with fasting :
Includes Water/Juice/Smoothie/Lemonade

* Before starting any new program it is advised to consult your primary physician

Healthy benefits of cleansing

* Purifies the blood

* Creates better elimination, blood circulation

* Weight management

* Promotes healthy, glowing skin

* Supports organ function

* Increases memory & focus

* Stimulates energy

* Supports libido

* Creates more flexibility

* Builds stronger immune system

* Slows down the aging process

A. CLEANSING & DETOXIFYING DRINKS

1. SOUR SPICE

MUCUS CLEANSER DETOX DRINK
SERVING : 2 CUPS

INGREDIENTS :

WATER = 2 CUPS
LEMON = 1 WHOLE SQUEEZE IT
GINGER = 1-2 INCHES
MAPLE SYRUP/HONEY = 1-2 TBSPS
CILANTRO = 1-2 PIECES

Count :

Cal = 107 / cup
Carb = 21 g / cup
Sugar (fructose) = 8 g / cup
Ca = 10 mg / cup
Mg = 7.5 mg / cup

Benefits :

* Detoxifies the body
* Maintains the PH balance
* Strengthens the immune system
* Improves weight loss * Creates radiant skin

Simple Steps :

Wash, cut and peel the ingredients and place in the blender.
Enjoy it !

2. GRAPE GOODNESS

Fresh parsley-grape drink is a great power tool to detox the whole entire body.

Serving : 2 cups

Ingredients :

Grapes (with seeds) = 2 cups
Water = 1 cup
Fresh parsley = 1-2 sticks

Count :

Cal = 60 /cup
Carb = 14 g / cup
Sugar (fructose) = 11 g / cup
Ca = 33 mg / cup
Mg = 12 mg / cup

Benefits :

* Helps weight management
* Speeds up the metabolism
* Full of antioxidants (protects the cells, skin)
* Supports digestion
* Boosts the immune system
* Helps to reduce the water retention and bloating
* Balances blood sugar

Simple Steps :

Place all ingredients ink the blender and liquify it for 1-2 minutes.

3. MINTY MELON

Serving : 2 cups

Ingredients :

Water melon (with seeds) = 2 cups
Flax seeds (ground) = 1-2 tbsps
Fresh mint = 6-7 leaves
Lemon = 1/2 squeeze it
Water = 1 cup

Count :
Cal = 81 / cup

Carb = 11 g / cup
Sodium = 3 mg / cup
Potassium = 215 mg / cup
Sugar (fructose)= 7 g / cup
Ca = 11 mg / cup
Mg = 15 mg / cup

Benefits :

* Excellent hydratation
* Skin clarity & hair strength
* Better digestion
* Metabolism booster
* Balances the PH level
* Contains Omega 3 essential oil
(supports cardiac function)
* Contains antioxidants, vitamins & minerals
* High in fiber
* Reduces gastritis

Simple Steps :

Wash, cut and place all ingredients in the blender.

4. COCO SPINACH

Serving : 2 cups

Ingredients :
Grapes (with seeds)= 2 cups
Spinach = 1 hand full
Coconut water = 1 cup (8 oz)
Water = 1 cup

Count :

Cal = 135 / cup
Carb = 19 g / cup
Sugar (fructose) = 28 g / cup
Sodium = 70 mg / cup
Potassium = 520 mg / cup
Ca = 55 mg / cup
Mg = 23 mg / cup

Benefits :

* Promotes better digestion
* Boosts metabolism
* Balances blood sugar and pressure
* Cleanses the kidneys
* Immune booster
* Nourishes the bones and muscles
* Flushes free radicals
* Full of nutrients, antioxidants, fiber, vitamins, minerals and potassium
* Great hydration

Simple Steps :

Wash and place all ingredients in the blender.

B. ENERGY BOOSTER

SMOOTHIES AND BITES

" THOSE WHO HAVE NO TIME FOR HEALTHY
EATING WILL SOONER OR LATER
HAVE TO FIND TIME FOR ILLNESS. "

- Edward Stanley -

1. IRON BANANA

EXCELLENT PRE-WORKOUT SMOOTHIE AND GREAT SOURCE OF ENERGY.

Serving : 2 cups

Ingredients :
Banana = 1 ripe one
Hemp seeds = 2 tbsps
Coconut wager = 1 cup (8oz)
Spinach = 1 hand full
Soaked dates = 2 - 4
Water = 1 cup

Count:

Cal = 153 / cup
Carb = 18 g / cup
Sodium = 50 mg / cup
Potassium = 465 mg / cup
Sugar (fructose) = 8 g / cup
Protein = 5 g / cup
Ca = 18 mg / cup
Mg = 95 mg / cup
Phosphorus = 180 mg / cup

Benefits :

* Excellent source of potassium
(balances blood pressure)
* Promotes better circulation, heart, mood, kidney, vision
and brain function
* Improves digestion
* Boosts energy

Simple Steps :

Place all ingredients in the blender and liquify it.

2. TURMERIC MANGO

Serving : 2 cups

Ingredients :

Banana = 1 ripe one
Flax seeds (ground) = 1 tbsps
Coconut water = 1 cup
Mango = 1 small
Turmeric = a hint
Cinnamon = a hint
Water = 1 cup
Dates (soaked) = 2 - 4

Count :

Cal = 275 / cup
Carb = 35 g / cup
Sodium = 53 mg / cup
Potassium = 930 mg / cup
Sugar (fructose) = 25 g / cup
Ca = 68 mg / cup
Mg = 77 mg / cup
Phosphorus = 79 mg / cup

Benefits :

* Provides vitamins, minerals and fiber
* Supports digestion and circulation
* Balances heart functions
* Improves mood
* Supports kidney and brain function
* Improves vision
* Lowers blood pressure
* Balances blood sugar and cholesterol

Simple Steps :

Wash, peel, cut the ingredients and place them in the blender.

3. CREAMY COCONUT

Rich in creamy coconut meat, water and banana.

Serving : 2 cups

Ingredients :

Banana = 1 ripe one
Coconut water = 1 cup
Shredded coconut = 1 - 2 tbsps
Flax seeds (ground) = 2 tbsps
Dates (soaked) = 2 - 4
Water = 1 cup

Count :

Cal = 237 / cup
Carb = 28 g / cup
Sodium = 53 mg / cup
Potassium = 689 mg / cup
Sugar (fructose) = 25g / cup
Ca = 61 mg / cup
Mg = 68 mg / cup
Phosphorus = 13 mg / cup

Benefits :

* Eliminates sugar cravings.
* Rich in vitamins, minerals, fiber and antioxidants.

Simple Steps :

Wash, cut and place all ingredients in the blender.

4. VERY CHERRY

Powerful energy booster and fat burner drink.

Serving : 2 cups

Ingredients :

Cherry = 1 cup
Coconut water = 1 cup
Avocado = 1/2
Dates (soaked) = 2 - 4 big ones
Water = 1 cup
Goji berry = 2 oz

Count :

Cal = 235 / cup
Carb = 35 g / cup
Potassium = 687 mg / cup
Sugar (fructose) = 25 g / cup
Protein = 7 g / cup
Ca = 80 mg / cup
Mg = 28 mg / cup

Benefits :

* Anti-inflammatory
* Good source of hydration
* Supports weight management
* Improves digestion
* Boosts metabolic function
* Fat burning catalyst

Simple Steps :

Place all ingredients (washed, cut) in the blender.

5. KEY-LIME DARK CHOCOLATE ENERGY

BITES

Serving : 14 -15 balls
(1bite = 1.6 oz)

Ingredients :

Oats (quick) = 1.5 cups
Pistachio (raw, shelled) = 2 oz
Coconut water = 4 oz (with citrus juice)
Coconut oil = 1 tbsp
Rasins = 4 oz
Cranberry = 2 oz
Pink Himalayan salt = a hint
Lime = 1/2 - 1 juice

Lemon = 1/2 shred the skin+juice
Turmeric = a hint
Flax seeds (ground) = 1 tbsps

Count :

Cal = 90
Carb = 14 g
Sugar (fructose) = 5 g
Protein = 2 g
Sodium = 4 g
Potassium = 87 mg
Ca = 10 mg
Mg = 4.5 mg
Phosphorus = 8.7 mg

Benefits :

* Energy booster
* Alkalizes the body
* Speeds up the metabolism
* Improves bone strength
* Reduces appetite
* Creates a beautiful glowing skin
* Builds immune system

Simple Steps :

Place all ingredients in the blender, except oats.
Mix the blended ingredients with the oats in a separate dish.
Use a fork.

Create those balls with the ice cream scoop
(1.6 oz)

Reshape them with your hands.
Individually dip the balls in the oats in a separate soup dish
and shape them by hands.

When all bites are formed and ready, dip them in (low
heated) melted chocolate 1/2 way or fully.

Place them on a tray/dish on a wax paper.

Cool them in the fridge/freezer for 10-15 minutes and
enjoy them.

6. SPINACH ENERGY BITES

Replaces dependance on caffeine and candy sugar for energy.

Serving : 14 -15 bites
(1.6 oz)

Ingredients :

Oats (quick) = 1.5 cup
Spinach (fresh) = 1 hand full

Raw almond (shredded) = 2 oz
Coconut water = 3 oz
Coconut oil = 1 tbsps
Raisins = 2 oz blender + 2 oz dish
Pink Himalayan salt = a hint
Flax seeds (ground) = 1 tbsps
Spirulina = 1/2 tsp

Count :

Cal = 85
Carb = 12 g
Sugar (fructose) = 5 g
Protein = 2 g
Sodium = 8 mg
Potassium = 76 mg
Phosphorus = 12 mg
Ca = 8 mg
Mg = 6 mg

Benefits :

* High in fiber, antioxidants, vitamins and minerals
* Increases brain function
* Contains anti aging properties

* Creates better vision
* Reduces appetite
* Promotes weight management

Simple Steps :

Place all items in the blender except oats.
Mix the blended ingredients with the oats in a separate dish.
Use a fork.

Creates balls with the ice cream scoop.
Reshape them with your hands.

Individually dip them in the oats and shape them again.
When all balls are formed and ready, dip them in (low
heated), melted, dark, vegan chocolate
1/2 way or fully.

Place them on a tray/dish on a wax paper.

Cool them in the fridge/freezer for 10-15 minutes and
enjoy the taste.

C. MEAL REPLACEMENT :

SMOOTHIES AND BARS

" THE EASIEST DIET IS,
YOU KNOW,
EAT VEGETABLES,
EAT FRESH FOOD.
JUST A REALLY SENSIBLE HEALTHY DIET
LIKE YOU
READ ABOUT ALL THE TIME. "

- Drew Carey -

* Are you always own the run?
* Are you always in a hurry?
* Not enough time to eat healthy?

There is an easy solution!

Guru Girl's MEAL REPLACEMENT
Smoothies and Multi seeds bars are
PACKED
with vital Nutritions,
Antioxidants,
Minerals,
Vitamins and Healthy Calories.

These recipes Will help SUPPRESS your Appetite,
ENERGIZE the body and
help you ACHIEVE greater health.

1. PINEAPPLE PARADISE

An excellent immune system booster.

Serving : 2 cups

Ingredients :
Pineapple = 2 cups
Hemp seed = 1 - 2 tbsp
Cucumber = 1/2 big one
Banana = 1
Grapes = 1 cup
Coconut water = 1 cup
Water = 1/2 cup
Vegan powder shake = 1- 2 scoops
(your favorite)

Count :
Cal = 365 / cup
Carb = 45 g / cup
Potassium = 895 mg / cup
Sugar (fructose) = 37 g / cup
Protein = 25 g / cup
Folate = 45 mcg / cup
Ca = 75 mg / cup
Mg = 124 mg / cup
Iron = 8 mg / cup
Phosphorus = 215 mg / cup

Benefits :
* Anti - inflammatory
* Weight management
* Maintains digestion
* High in antioxidants, vitamins and minerals
* Supports vision, heart function and circulation
* Lowers cholesterol
* Assistes kidney function

Simple Steps :
Wash, cut and place all ingredients in the blender.
Liquify it for 1-2 minutes.
Enjoy the taste of it!

2. V- 4

A combination of vegetables and fruits.

Serving : 2 cups

Ingredients :
Spinach = 1 handfull
Apple juice = 1 cup
Celery = 1 stalk
Apple juice = 1 cup
Carrots = 1/2
Cucumber = 1/2
Hemp seeds = 1 - 2 tbsp
Water = 1 cup
Vegan protein powder = 1- 2 scoops
(your favorite)

Count :
Cal = 228 / cup
Carb = 23 g / cup
Potassium = 340 mg / cup
Sugar (fructose) = 15 g / cup
Protein = 29 g / cup
Vitamin A = 7,567 IU / cup
Vitamin C = 26 mg / cup
Ca = 111 mg / cup
Mg = 81 mg / cup
Iron = 8 mg / cup
Phosphorus = 195 mg / cup

Benefits :
* Rich in minerals, vitamins, nutrients, fiber, protein, Ca,
Folate, Zinc, Beta-carotene and Flavonoids
* Improves memory
* Lowers blood pressure and sugar level
* Supports vision and kidney function
* Weight management
* Hydration

Simple Steps :
Place all washed, cut ingredients in the blender and Bon
Appetite! Drink it slowly, enjoy and taste every drop.

3. SUPER SEEDS & NUTS POWER BARS

Serving :15 bars /
each 2.5 oz

Ingredients :
Raw almond(shredded) = 4 oz
Sunflower seeds = 4 oz
Pumpkin Seeds = 4 oz
Cashew = 4 oz
Flax seeds = 4 oz
Pistachio = 4 oz
Walnuts = 4 oz
Chia seeds = 4 oz
Rasins = 4 oz
Flax seed (ground) = 2 tbsps
Cranberry = 2 oz
Goji berry = 2 oz
lemon juice = few drops
Cinnamon = hint
Pink Himalayan salt = 1/4 tsp
Cayenne pepper = hint (optional)
Vanilla extra = few drops
Apple juice = 4 oz
Fresh ginger or ginger powder = hint (optional) or 1-2 inches

Count / bar :
Cal = 250
Carb = 15 g
Protein = 9 g
Total Fat = 18 g
Saturated Fat = 2 g
Sugar (fructose) = 5 g

Benefits :
* Provides high energy
* Creates high level of muscle building 9 g of protein/ serving
* Alkalize the body
* Rich in vitamins, minerals and essential oils
* Contains healthy calories
* Lowers cholesterol

Simple Steps :
Place all ingredients in the food processor, blend them gently for 1-2 minutes.
Shape the paste in a mold.
Refrigerate it for 30 minutes and enjoy the healthy protein bars.

D. MUSCLE BUILDER & REJUVENATING

SMOOTHIES AND BARS

" Some people are willing to pay the price and it's the same

with staying healthy or eating healthy.

There's some discipline involved.

There's some sacrifices. "

- Mike Ditka -

1. RASPBERRY RED

A rejuvenator and muscle builder elixir.
Serving : 2 cups

Ingredients :
Banana = 1
Raspberry = 1 cup
Spinach = 1 handfull
Coconut water = 1 cup
Coconut oil = 1 tbsp
Maple syrup = 1/2 - 1 tbsp
Water = 1 cup
Vegan protein powder = 1- 2 scoops
(your favorite)

Count :

Cal = 243 / cup
Carb = 29 g / cup
Sodium = 232 mg / cup
Potassium = 462 g / cup
Sugar = 19 g / cup
Ca = 101 mg / cup
Mg = 28 mg / cup
Protein = 12 g / cup
Iron = 7 mg / cup

Benefits :

* Perfect combination of antioxidants, protein, Ca, Mg,
Zinc
* Contributes weight management
* Supports immune system
* Creates a healthier and younger looking body and skin

Simple Steps :

Wash, cut and place all ingredients in the blender. Liquify it
and slowly drink it up.

2. CREAMY CHOCOLATE

A delicious chocolate and berry flavor post workout
smoothie.
Serving : 2 cups

Ingredients :
Kale = 1 handful
Avocado = 1/2
Mixed berries = 1 cup
Coconut water = 1 cup
Water = 1/2 cup
Raw cacao powder = 1/2 - 1tbsp
Rasins = 1oz
Celery = 2 sticks
Cranberry = 1 oz
Vegan protein powder = 1 - 2 scoops

Count :
Cal = 271 / cup
Carb = 39 g / cup
Sugar (fructose) = 27 g / cup
Sodium = 104 mg / cup
Potassium = 836 g / cup
Protein = 7 g / cup
Ca = 135 mg / cup
Mg = 87 mg / cup

Benefits :
* Contains 12 g of protein
* Rich in vitamin A, C, K, B, C, folate and omega 3 fatty acids
* Lowers cholesterol
* Builds muscle tissues
* Protect the heart great energy booster

Simple Steps :
Place all ingredients in the blender and enjoy it.

3. PEANUT-BUTTER PROTEIN BARS

Serving : 6 -7 bars

Ingredients :
Oats = 1.5 cups
Peanuts = 2 oz
Peanut-butter = 1- 2 big tbsp
Coconut water = 3 oz + 1 oz water
Coconut oil = 1 tbsp
Rasins = 4 oz
Flaxseed (ground) = 1 tbsp
Barley malt = 1/2 - 1 tbsp
Pink himalayan salt = hint
Vegan protein powder = 1- 2 scoops
Dark vegan chocolate = 2 oz (mix it), 1/2-1 cup to dip it
(optional)

Count :
Cal = 275/ bar

Carb = 28 / bar
Sugar = 11 g / bar
Protein = 17 g / bar
Iron = 4 g / bar
Ca = 23 mg / bar
Mg = 21 g / bar

Benefits :
* Great energy source
* Excellent workout meal
* Contains healthy fats
* With the added oats it lowers cholesterol
* Supports better focus and concentration
* Each bar is packed with 10-12 g of protein, vitamins, minerals and antioxidants
* Controls weight management
* Balance blood sugar and pressure

Simple Steps :
Place all ingredients in the blender except oats.
Mix the paste with the oats in a separate bowl.
Use a fork.
Place it in the mold.
Refrigerate it for 30 minutes and dip half into melted chocolate.

4. KEY-LIME PROTEIN BARS
Excellent post workout meal
(30 minutes after exercise)

Serving : 6 - 7 bars / 1 bar = 2.6 oz

Ingredients :
Oats = 1.5 cups
Coconut water = 4 oz with the lemon juice + 1 oz water
Coconut oil = 1 tbsp
Pistachio = 2 oz
Pink Himalayan salt = hint
Cranberry = 2 oz
Rasins = 4 oz
Turmeric = hint
Lime (1/2) = shred the skin + juice
Lemon (1/2) = shred the skin + juice
Flaxseed (ground) = 1 tbsp
Vegan protein powder (vegan) =1 - 2 scoops

Vegan dark chocolate = 1/2-1 cup to melt and dip it (optional)

Count :
Cal = 275 / bar
Carb = 35 g / bar
Sugar = 15 g / bar
Protein = 10 g / bar
Ca = 47 mg / bar
Mg = 12 mg / bar
Iron = 4 mg / bar

Benefits :
* Protects the muscles
* Reduces inflammation
* Boosts energy, immune system, digestive system
* Weight management
* Lowers cholesterol, blood sugar and pressure
* Full of nutrients

Simple Steps :
Place all ingredients (except oats) in the blender and liquify it.Mix it all in a separate bowl with the oats. Use a fork.
Place the paste in the mold.
Cool it down in the freezer for 15 - 20 minutes.
Deep one side in chocolate and enjoy it. (optional)

VII. SIMPLE STEPS TO LEARN HOW TO EAT

HEALTHY

1., To begin with discard all unhealthy, artificial meals, snacks and ingredients from your kitchen (fridge, freezer and cabinets)

2., Replace them with all natural, fresh or frozen, organic and healthy foods, ingredients.

3., Preparation includes making a grocery list, because it helps to stay focused. It saves time and creates peace of mind.

4., Eating a healthy meal prior to grocery shopping helps prevent random and erratic shopping of unhealthy and unnecessary items.

5., Feel free to customize these recipes, be creative and enjoy your journey in the kitchen.

1. UNHEALTHY EATING HABITS :

- EATING TOO FAST ,

- SPEAKING CONSTANTLY WHILE EATING ,

- WATCHING TV, TALKING ON THE PHONE ,

- NOT SITTING CALMLY ,

- NOT THOROUGHLY CHEWING THE FOOD ,

- NOT SAVORING IT ,

- OVER EATING OF DUE TO STRESS ,

- NOT EATING AT ALL OF DUE TO STRESS .

2. CONCLUSION :

* I BELIEVE AS IN PRAYER AND MEDITATION IT IS IMPORTANT TO SIT QUIETLY AND WITHOUT DISTRACTIONS WHILE EATING .

* THIS ENABLES US TO MAKE OUR MEAL INTO A SPIRITUAL EXPERIENCE .

* THIS IS ACCOMPLISHED BY INVOKING ALL OUR SENSES (AUDIO, VISUAL, TOUCH, SMELL AND TASTE) AND MAXIMIZING OUR EXPERIENCE .

* BY SLOWING DOWN, CHEWING OUR FOOD 20-30 TIMES, MIXING IT WELL WITH THE SALIVA WHICH ENABLES BETTER DIGESTION .

* TRY TO INCORPORATE THESE TIPS INTO YOUR DAILY ROUTINE AND YOU WILL EXPERIENCE THE DIFFERENCE .

" HEALTHY EATING IS A WAY OF LIFE ,
SO IT ' S IMPORTANT TO ESTABLISH
ROUTINES THAT ARE SIMPLE , REALISTICALLY
AND ULTIMATELY LIVABLE . "

- ARTHUR AGATSTON -

ABOUT THE AUTHOR

ANDREA NOEMI BREDAK WAS BORN IN
BUDAPEST , HUNGARY .

SHE IS AN ENTHUSIASTIC INSTRUCTOR ,
TEACHER AND MENTOR
TO PEOPLE .

ANDREA HAS A DEEP PASSION
FOR FOOD AND EXERCISE .
WITH HER UNIQUE STYLE
SHE TEACHES STRETCHING ,
DANCE , MINDFULNESS , MOVEMENTS AND
MEDITATION .

HER TECHNIQUE SPECIFIC
TO THE HIGHEST LEVEL OF THE CLASS .
HIGHLY MOTIVATED TO GUIDE EACH AND
EVERY INDIVIDUAL TO REACH THEIR HEALTH
AND FITNESS GOALS .

PROMOTES ACTIVITIES AND COPING METHODS
TO TRANSFORM OLD HABITS AND FUEL
HEALTHY BODIES , MIND AND SOUL .

ENJOY THE JOURNEY .
GREAT HEALTH, JOY AND LOVE .

EMAIL : GURUGIRLSTORE@YAHOO.COM
INSTAGRAM : GURUGIRLLIFE
FB.: GURU GIRL